101 Things® To Do With Pancake Mix

Yum!

**More recipes and tips
at 101yum.com**

101 Things® To Do With Pancake Mix

BY
STEPHANIE ASHCRAFT

GIBBS SMITH
TO ENRICH AND INSPIRE HUMANKIND

To our neighbors and the great people of the
town of Marana. Thank you for all you do.

First Edition
15 14 13 12 11   5 4 3 2 1

Published by
Gibbs Smith
P.O. Box 667
Layton, Utah 84041

1.800.835.4993 orders
www.gibbs-smith.com

Printed and bound in Korea

Gibbs Smith books are printed on either recycled, 100% post-consumer
waste, FSC-certified papers or on paper produced from sustainable PEFC-
certified forest/controlled wood source. Learn more at www.pefc.org.

Library of Congress Cataloging-in-Publication Data

Ashcraft, Stephanie.
   101 things to do with pancake mix / Stephanie Ashcraft. — 1st ed.
      p. cm.
   ISBN 978-1-4236-0790-8
   1. Quick and easy cooking. 2. Pancakes, waffles, etc. 3. Cookbooks.
   I. Title. II. Title: One hundred and one things to do with pancake mix.
   III. Title: One hundred one things to do with pancake mix.
   TX833.5.A84 2011
   641.8'15—dc22

                        2010052569

CONTENTS

Waffles

Other Breakfast Sensations

Dinner Dishes

Desserts

Helpful Hints 126

SYRUPS & TOPPINGS

Apple Syrup

1/4 cup	**brown sugar**
2 tablespoons	**cornstarch**
1/4 teaspoon	**ground allspice**
1/8 teaspoon	**ground nutmeg**
1 3/4 cups	**apple juice**

In a 2-quart saucepan, combine brown sugar, cornstarch, allspice, and nutmeg. Whisk in apple juice. Cook over medium heat, stirring often, until bubbly and syrup starts to thicken. Makes 1 3/4 cups.

Maple Syrup

1 cup	**water**
1 cup	**sugar**
1 cup	**brown sugar**
2 teaspoons	**maple extract**

In a 2-quart saucepan, combine water and sugars. Bring to a boil. Boil for 2–3 minutes. Stir in extract. Makes 1 cup.

Buttermilk Syrup

1 cup	**sugar**
1/4 cup	**butter or margarine**
1/2 cup	**buttermilk**
1 tablespoon	**light corn syrup**
1/2 teaspoon	**baking soda**
1/2 teaspoon	**vanilla**

In a 2-quart saucepan, combine sugar, butter, buttermilk, syrup, and baking soda. Bring to a boil. Boil for 2–3 minutes, stirring constantly. Remove from heat and stir in vanilla. Allow syrup to cool for 5 minutes. Makes 1 cup.

Cinnamon Syrup

I cup	**light corn syrup**
I ½ cups	**sugar**
½ cup	**water**
½ tablespoon	**cinnamon**
I cup	**evaporated milk**

In a 2-quart saucepan, combine syrup, sugar, water, and cinnamon. Bring to a boil. Boil for 2 minutes, stirring constantly. Remove from heat. Let stand for 2 minutes and stir in milk. Makes 2 cups.

Mixed-Berry Syrup

I cup	**sugar**
I ½ tablespoons	**cornstarch**
¾ cup	**water**
I ½ cups	**frozen mixed berries**

In a 2-quart saucepan, combine sugar and cornstarch. Stir in water. Add berries. Bring to a boil, stirring constantly until syrup begins to thicken. Makes 2½ cups.

Orange Sauce

½ cup	**sugar**
I tablespoon	**cornstarch**
pinch	**salt**
¾ cup	**water**
I tablespoon	**butter or margarine**
⅓ cup	**frozen orange juice concentrate,** thawed

In a I-quart saucepan, stir together sugar, cornstarch, and salt. Whisk in water and butter and bring to a boil, stirring constantly. Add juice and bring syrup back to a boil, stirring until it thickens. Makes I½ cups.

Maple Cream Topping

1 cup	**pure maple syrup**
1/2 cup	**whipping cream**
2 tablespoons	**butter or margarine**

In a 2-quart saucepan, combine syrup, cream, and butter. Bring to a boil, stirring constantly. Reduce heat and continue to cook at a boil for 4–5 minutes, stirring constantly to assure that it doesn't boil over. Makes 1 1/2 cups.

Praline Syrup

1 cup	**dark corn syrup**
3 tablespoons	**brown sugar**
1/4 cup	**water**
1/2 cup	**coarsely chopped pecans**
1/2 teaspoon	**vanilla**

In a 2-quart saucepan, combine syrup, brown sugar, and water. Bring to a boil and boil for 1 minute. Remove from heat and stir in pecans and vanilla. Makes 1 1/2 cups.

Raspberry Syrup

1 cup	**fresh raspberries**
1/3 cup	**water**
3 tablespoons	**sugar**
1 tablespoon	**cornstarch**
1 teaspoon	**lemon juice**

In a 2-quart saucepan, add berries and water. In a small bowl, combine sugar and cornstarch. Sprinkle sugar mixture over raspberries in pan. Stir in lemon juice. Cook over medium-high heat, stirring constantly, until syrup comes to a boil and thickens. Remove from heat. Makes 1 1/4 cups.

Coconut Syrup

1 cup	**milk**
2 tablespoons	**butter or margarine**
4 drops	**coconut extract**
¾ cup	**sugar**
1 tablespoon	**cornstarch**
⅛ teaspoon	**salt**
½ teaspoon	**vanilla**

In a 2-quart saucepan, heat milk, butter, and coconut extract until butter melts. In a 1-quart bowl, stir together sugar, cornstarch, and salt. Slowly stir sugar mixture into milk mixture. Bring to a boil for 2 minutes. Remove from heat and stir in vanilla. Store leftover syrup in the refrigerator. Makes 1¼ cups.

Blueberry Sauce

1½ cups	**fresh or frozen blueberries**
7 tablespoons	**water,** divided
¾ cup	**orange juice**
½ cup	**sugar**
2 tablespoons and ½ teaspoon	**cornstarch**
¼ teaspoon	**vanilla or almond extract**
¼ teaspoon	**ground cinnamon**

In a 2-quart saucepan, combine berries, 3 tablespoons water, juice, and sugar. Stir occasionally and gently until sauce comes to a boil. In a small bowl, whisk together cornstarch and remaining water. Gently stir cornstarch mixture into berries. Simmer for an additional 3–4 minutes until sauce begins to thicken. Remove from heat and stir in extract and cinnamon. Makes 2 cups.

APPETIZERS & ENTERTAINING

PILED-HIGH
VEGETABLE RANCH PIZZA

2³⁄₄ cups	**pancake mix**
²⁄₃ cup	**very hot water**
I package (8 ounces)	**cream cheese,** softened
I container (6 ounces)	**non-fat Greek plain yogurt**
¹⁄₂ envelope (1.125 ounces)	**ranch salad dressing mix**
	carrots, cucumber, red bell pepper, broccoli, tomatoes, and/or green onions, sliced or diced
I can (2.25 ounces)	**sliced black olives,** drained
¹⁄₂ cup	**grated sharp cheddar cheese**

Preheat oven to 350 degrees.

In a 2-quart bowl, combine pancake mix and water until dough forms.
Use hands to work pancake mix completely into the dough. Spread
dough into a 9 x 13-inch pan prepared with nonstick cooking spray.
Bake for 15 minutes. Allow crust to completely cool.

In a 2-quart bowl, mix together cream cheese and yogurt until
smooth. Stir in dressing mix. Spread cream cheese mixture evenly over
cooled crust. Top with desired amount of vegetables. Evenly distribute
olives and cheese over pizza. Refrigerate until ready to serve. Makes
15 servings.

CHEESY JALAPENO PANCAKE BITES

2 cups	**pancake mix**
1 1/4 cups	**water**
1/2 cup	**ranch salad dressing**
I can (4 ounces)	**diced jalapeno peppers,** drained
2 cups	**grated mozzarella cheese**
	salsa
	ranch salad dressing

Heat an electric griddle to 350 degrees and prepare with nonstick cooking spray.

In a 2-quart bowl, combine pancake mix, water, and ranch dressing. Stir in jalapenos and cheese. Using a 2 tablespoon-size cookie scoop, drop batter evenly spaced over top of griddle. Cook for 2–3 minutes and flip to cook on the other side. Cook until second side is golden brown. Serve each pancake bite warm with a spoonful of salsa and a drizzle of dressing over the top. Makes 30 bites.

ITALIAN SAUSAGE MINI ROLLS

3 cups	**pancake mix**
1 pound	**ground sausage**
4 cups	**grated mozzarella cheese**
1/2 cup	**grated Parmesan cheese**
1/2 cup	**milk**
2 teaspoons	**Italian seasoning**
	barbecue sauce or honey mustard

Preheat oven to 350 degrees.

In a 2-quart bowl, combine pancake mix, raw sausage, cheeses, milk, and seasoning. Knead the dough with your hands until all the pancake mix is worked in. Prepare 2 baking sheets with nonstick cooking spray. Use a 1 tablespoon-size cookie scoop to drop small balls of dough onto the baking sheet. Bake for 17–23 minutes. Dip baked mini rolls in barbecue sauce or honey mustard. Makes 38–40 appetizers.

7-LAYER HOT BEAN DIP

I can (16 ounces)	**black bean refried beans**
I ⅓ cups	**salsa,** divided
I can (4 ounces)	**chopped green chiles,** with liquid
I cup	**pancake mix**
¾ cup	**grated cheddar cheese**
I cup	**shredded lettuce**
¼ cup	**chopped onion**
I	**tomato,** seeded and diced
½ container (6 ounces)	**plain yogurt**
	tortilla chips

Preheat oven to 375 degrees.

In a 2-quart bowl, combine refried beans, ⅓ cup salsa, chiles, and pancake mix. Spread mixture into an 8 x 8-inch pan prepared with nonstick cooking spray. Spoon remaining salsa over bean layer. Sprinkle cheese over top. Bake for 30 minutes. Remove from oven and allow to cool for 5 minutes. Layer lettuce, onion, tomato, and yogurt over hot bean dip. Serve immediately with tortilla chips. Makes 8–10 servings.

QUICK HUSHPUPPIES

	vegetable or canola oil
1 box (8.5 ounces)	**corn muffin mix**
1 cup	**pancake mix**
1 can (14.75 ounces)	**cream-style corn**
3 tablespoons	**chopped green onion**

Heat oil in deep fryer or 4-quart saucepan to 375 degrees.

In a 2-quart bowl, combine muffin mix, pancake mix, and corn. Stir in onion. Drop tablespoons of dough into hot oil. Fry for 2–4 minutes until golden brown. Place cooked hush puppies on plate covered with paper towels to drain. Makes 36–38 hushpuppies.

INDIVIDUAL BACON SWISS QUICHES

Crust:

1/2 cup	**butter or margarine,** melted
2 cups	**pancake mix**
1	**egg**

Filling:

1/2 cup	**cooked and crumbled bacon**
1/4 cup	**chopped green onions**
1/2 cup	**grated Swiss cheese**
2	**eggs**
3/4 cup	**evaporated milk**
1/4 teaspoon	**pepper**

Preheat oven to 325 degrees.

To make the crust; combine butter, pancake mix, and egg in a 2-quart bowl until dough is formed. Prepare a 12-cup muffin pan with nonstick cooking spray. Using a 2 tablespoon-size cookie scoop, drop balls of dough into each muffin cup. Divide any remaining dough between the 12 cups. Press the dough along the bottom and up the sides of each muffin cup. Spoon 2 teaspoons bacon into each cup and then sprinkle in 1 teaspoon onion followed by 2 teaspoons cheese.

In a 1-quart bowl, whisk together eggs, milk, and pepper until well blended. Spoon 2 tablespoons egg mixture into each cup. Divide any remaining egg mixture evenly between the 12 cups. Bake for 22–28 minutes until eggs are set. Allow quiches to cool in the pan for 5 minutes. Run a sharp knife around the edge of quiches. Remove and set the quiches on a serving platter. Makes 12 quiches.

ONION RINGS

	vegetable or canola oil
1	extra large white onion
2 cups	pancake mix
1½ cups	water
½ teaspoon	salt

Heat oil in deep fryer or 4-quart saucepan to 375 degrees.

Remove the end of the onion and outer layer. Slice the onion crosswise and separate into rings. In a large shallow bowl, beat pancake mix, water, and salt together. Batter will be slightly lumpy. Dip onion rings into the batter, coating as much as possible, and drop in the hot oil and fry until golden brown. Place onion rings on a plate covered with paper towels to drain. Serve with dipping sauce of your choice. Makes 3–4 servings.

FRENCH-FRIED PICKLES

	vegetable or canola oil
2	**eggs,** slightly beaten
⅓ cup	**milk**
2 tablespoons	**pickle juice**
¾ cup	**pancake mix**
1 teaspoon	**lemon pepper**
1 jar (16 ounces)	**Vlasic Stackers pickles**
	ranch dressing

Heat oil in deep fryer or 4-quart saucepan to 375 degrees.

In a 2-quart bowl, combine eggs, milk, and pickle juice. Whisk in pancake mix and lemon pepper until smooth. Pat dry pickle slices with a paper towel and then dip into batter. Fry slices in hot oil until golden brown. Place fried pickles on a plate covered with paper towels to drain. Serve hot as an appetizer or snack with ranch dressing. Makes 14 fried pickles.

FRUIT PIZZA

¹/₂ cup	**butter or margarine,** softened
1 ¹/₃ cups	**sugar,** divided
2	**eggs**
2 teaspoons	**vanilla,** divided
2 ¹/₂ cups	**pancake mix**
¹/₂ package (8 ounces)	**cream cheese,** softened
1 carton (half-pint)	**chilled whipping cream**
1 can (8 ounces)	**pineapple tidbits,** drained
1 can (11 ounces)	**mandarin oranges,** drained
¹/₂ cup	**blueberries**
1	**nectarine or peach,** peeled and diced
1 cup	**sliced strawberries**
¹/₂ cup	**toasted coconut,** optional

Preheat oven to 350 degrees.

To make the crust; cream together butter and 1 cup sugar in a 2-quart bowl until smooth. Mix in eggs, one at a time, and stir in 1 teaspoon vanilla. Stir in pancake mix until dough forms. Dough will be sticky. Spoon dough into a 9 x 13-inch pan prepared with nonstick cooking spray. Spray your hands with nonstick cooking spray and spread dough evenly over the bottom of the pan. Bake for 15–18 minutes until golden brown around edges. Using a metal serving spatula, pat the hot cookie crust flat. Allow crust to cool completely.

For the topping; using a 2-quart bowl, beat together cream cheese, remaining sugar, and remaining vanilla until smooth. Add whipping cream and beat until stiff peaks form. Spread evenly over cooled crust. Top with fruit. Sprinkle toasted coconut over the top, if desired. Refrigerate until ready to serve. Makes 15 servings.

FAIRGROUND BANANAS

	vegetable or canola oil
1 cup	**pancake mix**
¾ cup	**water**
3	**bananas,** cut into chunks
1½ teaspoons	**cinnamon**
½ cup	**sugar**

Heat oil in deep fryer or 4-quart saucepan to 340–350 degrees.

In a 1-quart bowl, whisk together pancake mix and water. Batter will be slightly lumpy. Coat banana chunks with pancake batter and fry in hot oil for 1–2 minutes on each side until golden brown. Combine cinnamon and sugar in a small bowl. Roll fried bananas in cinnamon-sugar mixture. Makes 3–4 servings.

APPLE FRITTERS

	vegetable or canola oil
4	**red or golden delicious apples**
2 teaspoons	**lemon juice**
2 cups	**pancake mix**
1 ½ cups	**water**
1 teaspoon	**cinnamon**
½ teaspoon	**nutmeg**
½ cup	**powdered sugar**

Heat oil in deep fryer or 4-quart saucepan to 340–350 degrees.

Peel, core, and slice apples into ¼-inch apple rings. Place apple rings in a shallow bowl. Sprinkle lemon juice evenly over apples.

In a 2-quart bowl, whisk together pancake mix, water, cinnamon, and nutmeg. Batter will be slightly lumpy. Coat apple slices in batter and fry in hot oil for 1–2 minutes on each side until golden brown. Place cooked fritters on a plate covered in paper towels. Sprinkle powdered sugar over fritters. Makes 20–24 apple fritters.

DONUT HOLES

	vegetable or canola oil
2⅔ cups	**pancake mix**
¾ cup	**sugar,** divided
1 cup	**water**
1	**egg**
1½ teaspoons	**cinnamon**

Heat oil in deep fryer or 4-quart saucepan to 350–375 degrees.

In a 2-quart bowl, combine pancake mix and ¼ cup of sugar. Add water and egg and stir until dough has formed. In a small bowl, combine remaining sugar and cinnamon.

Using a 1 tablespoon-size cookie scoop, drop balls of dough into hot oil. Fry for 1–2 minutes on each side until golden brown. Place cooked donut holes on a plate covered in paper towels. Roll donuts holes in cinnamon-sugar mixture before serving. Makes 35–40 donut holes.

BISCUITS, MUFFINS, & BREADS

CHEDDAR BISCUITS

5 cups	**pancake mix**
2/3 cup	**water**
1/2 cup	**butter or margarine,** melted
2	**eggs**
2 cups	**grated cheddar cheese**
1 tablespoon	**prepared mustard***

Preheat oven to 425 degrees.

In a 3-quart bowl, combine all ingredients until dough forms. Use a 3 tablespoon-size cookie scoop to drop balls of dough onto a baking sheet prepared with nonstick cooking spray. Bake 12–16 minutes. Makes 12–14 biscuits.

*1 teaspoon garlic powder can be used instead of prepared mustard.

SOUTHWEST BISCUITS

3 ½ cups	**pancake mix**
I tablespoon	**taco seasoning mix**
I can (10 ounces)	**diced tomatoes and green chiles,** drained
I cup	**milk**
I cup	**grated Mexican-blend cheese**

Preheat oven to 425 degrees.

In a 3-quart bowl, combine pancake mix and seasoning. Stir in tomatoes and chiles and milk. Fold in cheese. Use a 2 tablespoon-size cookie scoop to drop balls of dough onto baking sheet prepared with nonstick cooking spray. Bake for 11–14 minutes until golden. Makes 20 biscuits.

BERRY JAM MUFFINS

2 cups	**pancake mix**
2 tablespoons	**sugar**
1/2 cup	**butter or margarine**
1 cup	**milk**
1/4 cup	**strawberry or raspberry jam**

Topping:

1/4 cup	**butter or margarine,** softened
1/4 cup	**brown sugar**
1/3 cup	**quick oats**
1/4 cup	**flour**
1 teaspoon	**cinnamon**

Preheat oven to 425 degrees.

To make the muffins; combine pancake mix and sugar in a 2-quart bowl. Using a pastry cutter or fork, cut in butter until crumbly. Stir in milk until moistened. Line a muffin pan with paper liners or prepare with nonstick cooking spray. Spoon about 1 1/2 tablespoons of batter into each cup. Place 1 teaspoon jam in center of each muffin. Top with 1 teaspoon of remaining batter. Batter may not completely cover jam.

For the topping; using a 1-quart bowl, cream together butter and brown sugar. Stir in oats, flour, and cinnamon. Crumble topping evenly over muffins. Bake for 14–16 minutes. Cool muffins for 5 minutes before serving. Makes 12 muffins.

APPLE OATMEAL MUFFINS

1 ½ cups	**pancake mix**
1 cup	**oats**
½ cup	**brown sugar**
1 teaspoon	**ground cinnamon**
¾ cup	**milk**
⅓ cup	**canola or olive oil**
1	**egg**
1 teaspoon	**vanilla**
1 ½ cups	**peeled and chopped apples***

Preheat oven to 400 degrees.

In a 2-quart bowl, combine pancake mix, oats, brown sugar, and cinnamon. Stir in milk, oil, egg, and vanilla. Fold apples into batter. Line a muffin pan with paper liners or prepare with nonstick cooking spray. Evenly divide batter into muffin cups. Bake for 17–22 minutes. Makes 12 muffins.

*2 medium apples yield 1 ½ cups chopped apples.

BLUEBERRY MUFFINS

2 cups	**pancake mix**
1/2 cup	**ground flax seed**
1/2 cup	**sugar**
2/3 cup	**water**
1/4 cup	**canola or olive oil**
1	**egg**
1 package (6 ounces)	**blueberries**

Preheat oven to 400 degrees.

In a 2-quart bowl, combine pancake mix, flax seed, and sugar. Mix in water, oil, and egg. Batter will be slightly lumpy. Fold in blueberries. Line a muffin pan with paper liners or prepare with nonstick cooking spray. Fill muffin cups 2/3 full. Bake for 15–18 minutes. Makes 12 muffins.

CINNAMON AND SUGAR PANCAKE MUFFINS

2 cups	**pancake mix**
1/4 cup	**sugar**
1	**egg,** beaten
1 cup	**water**
1/4 cup	**Maple Syrup** (see page 7)

Topping:

1/4 cup	**sugar**
1 1/2 teaspoons	**cinnamon**
1 tablespoon	**butter or margarine,** melted and cooled

Preheat oven to 375 degrees.

To make the muffins; combine pancake mix and sugar in a 2-quart bowl. Stir in egg and water until combined. Stir in syrup. Line a muffin pan with paper liners or prepare with nonstick cooking spray. Fill each muffin cup halfway with batter. Distribute any remaining batter evenly over muffin cups.

For the topping; using a 1-quart bowl, combine sugar and cinnamon. Mix in butter until crumbly. Sprinkle a heaping 1/2 teaspoon cinnamon mixture evenly over top of each muffin. Bake for 18–23 minutes until done. Makes 12 muffins.

BANANA PRALINE MUFFINS

3	**small bananas,** mashed
1	**egg**
1/2 cup	**sugar**
1/4 cup	**canola or olive oil**
1 1/2 cups	**pancake mix**

Topping:

3 tablespoons	**butter or margarine,** melted and cooled
1/2 cup	**brown sugar**
1/2 cup	**chopped pecans**
1 tablespoon	**flour**

Preheat oven to 375 degrees.

To make the muffins; mix together bananas, egg, sugar, and oil in a 2-quart bowl until smooth. Stir in pancake mix. Line a muffin pan with paper liners or prepare with nonstick cooking spray and fill each cup 3/4 full.

For the topping; using a 1-quart bowl, combine butter and brown sugar. Stir in pecans and flour until crumbly. Distribute evenly over top of muffins. Bake for 18–20 minutes. Makes 12 muffins.

PUMPKIN
CHOCOLATE CHIP MUFFINS

2½ cups	**pancake mix**
½ cup	**sugar**
4 teaspoons	**pumpkin pie spice**
½ teaspoon	**salt**
½ cup	**water**
2	**eggs**
2 teaspoons	**vanilla**
1 cup	**canned pumpkin**
⅔ cup	**mini chocolate chips**

Preheat oven to 350 degrees.

In a 2-quart bowl, combine pancake mix, sugar, pumpkin pie spice, and salt. Add water, eggs, vanilla, and pumpkin and stir until moistened. Batter will be slightly lumpy. Fold in mini chocolate chips.

Line a muffin pan with paper liners or prepare with nonstick cooking spray. Fill muffin cups ⅔ full. Bake for 18–20 minutes. Makes 18 muffins.

VARIATION: Top baked muffins with chocolate frosting.

GREEN CHILE CORNBREAD

I cup	**pancake mix**
I cup	**cornmeal**
3 tablespoons	**sugar**
I cup	**milk**
¼ cup	**canola or olive oil**
I	**egg**
I can (4 ounces)	**diced green chiles**

Preheat oven to 400 degrees.

In a 2-quart bowl, combine pancake mix, cornmeal, and sugar. Stir in milk, oil, and egg. Batter will be slightly lumpy. Fold in green chiles. Pour batter into a 9 x 9-inch pan prepared with nonstick cooking spray. Bake for 18–20 minutes until done. Makes 9 servings.

DILL SWISS CHEESE BREAD

3 cups	**pancake mix**
2 tablespoons	**sugar**
1/4 cup	**finely chopped onion**
1 tablespoon	**dill seed**
1 1/2 cups	**milk**
1	**egg**
1 tablespoon	**canola or olive oil**
4 ounces	**Swiss cheese,** grated

Preheat oven to 350 degrees.

In a 2-quart bowl, combine pancake mix, sugar, onion, and dill. Stir in milk, egg, and oil until combined. Fold in cheese. Spread dough into an 8 x 4- or 9 x 5-inch bread pan liberally prepared with nonstick cooking spray. Bake for 40–45 minutes until golden brown. Allow to cool for 5–10 minutes before serving. Makes 6–8 servings.

APPLE NUT BREAD

I cup	**sugar**
¼ cup	**butter or margarine,** softened
2	**eggs**
I teaspoon	**cinnamon**
½ teaspoon	**ground cloves**
2 cups	**pancake mix**
2 cups	**peeled and chopped apples**
½ cup	**chopped pecans**

Preheat oven to 350 degrees.

In a 2-quart bowl, cream sugar and butter until smooth. Whisk in eggs, cinnamon, and cloves until smooth. Stir in pancake mix. Fold in apples and pecans. Spread dough into a 9 x 5-inch bread pan prepared with nonstick cooking spray. Bake for 55–60 minutes until golden brown. Makes 6–8 servings.

SWEET POTATO-
CRANBERRY PECAN LOAF

1 1/2 cups	**mashed sweet potatoes***
3/4 cup	**sugar**
1/2 cup	**milk**
1	**egg**
1 teaspoon	**cinnamon**
1/2 teaspoon	**nutmeg**
2 3/4 cups	**pancake mix**
1/2 cup	**finely chopped pecans**
1/2 cup	**dried cranberries**

Preheat oven to 350 degrees.

In a 2-quart bowl, mix together sweet potatoes, sugar, milk, egg, cinnamon, and nutmeg. Stir in pancake mix until dough is formed. Stir in pecans and cranberries. Spread dough into a 9 x 5-inch bread pan prepared with nonstick cooking spray. Bake for 45–50 minutes. Makes 6–8 servings.

* SHORTCUT: Drain 1 can (29 ounces) cut sweet potatoes or yams. Mash and measure 1 1/2 cups.

FRUITY
& FANCY
PANCAKES

APPLESAUCE PANCAKES

2 cups	**pancake mix**
1 ½ teaspoons	**pumpkin pie spice**
2	**eggs**
1 cup	**applesauce**
1 teaspoon	**lemon juice**
½ cup	**milk**
	applesauce or apple butter

Heat an electric griddle to 350 degrees. Prepare griddle with nonstick cooking spray.

In a 2-quart bowl, combine pancake mix and pumpkin pie spice. Stir in eggs, applesauce, lemon juice, and milk until well combined. Pour ¼ cup batter per pancake evenly onto hot griddle. Cook for 1–2 minutes on each side until golden brown. Serve with applesauce or apple butter spooned over top. Makes 12 pancakes.

VARIATION: Use wheat and honey pancake mix.

BANANA PANCAKES

2	**ripe bananas,** mashed
1 ½ cups	**water**
1 teaspoon	**vanilla**
2 cups	**pancake mix**
	Coconut Syrup (see page 10)
	or **Maple Syrup** (see page 7)

Heat an electric griddle to 350 degrees. Prepare griddle with nonstick cooking spray.

In a 2-quart bowl, combine bananas, water, and vanilla. Whisk pancake mix into banana mixture. Batter will be slightly lumpy. Pour ¼ cup batter per pancake evenly onto hot griddle. Cook for 1–2 minutes on each side until golden brown. Serve with Coconut Syrup or Maple Syrup. Makes 17–18 pancakes.

VARIATION: Stir ⅓ cup mini chocolate chips or chopped nuts into batter before cooking.

BLUEBERRY FLAX PANCAKES

1 ½ cups	**pancake mix**
½ cup	**ground flax seed**
1 ⅓ cups	**water**
1	**egg**
¾ cup	**fresh blueberries**
	Blueberry Sauce (see page 10)

Heat an electric griddle to 350 degrees. Prepare griddle with nonstick cooking spray.

In a 2-quart bowl, combine pancake mix and flax seed. In a 1-quart bowl, whisk together water and egg until smooth. Add the egg mixture to the pancake mix and whisk until combined. Carefully fold in blueberries. Pour ¼ cup batter per pancake evenly onto hot griddle. Cook for 1–2 minutes on each side until golden brown. Serve with Blueberry Sauce. Makes 10 pancakes.

BOYSENBERRY YOGURT PANCAKES

2 cups	**pancake mix**
1 cup	**water**
1 container (6 ounces)	**boysenberry yogurt**
	boysenberry syrup

Heat an electric griddle to 350 degrees. Prepare griddle with nonstick cooking spray.

In a 2-quart bowl, whisk together pancake mix, water, and yogurt. Batter will be slightly lumpy. Pour 1/4 cup batter per pancake evenly onto hot griddle. Cook for 1–2 minutes on each side until golden brown. Serve with boysenberry syrup. Makes 12 pancakes.

VARIATION: Try other flavor yogurts. Top with additional yogurt and fresh fruit to match flavor of yogurt used.

PANCAKE PIE FILLING STACKS

2 cups	**pancake mix**
1 ½ cups	**water**
1 container (24.3 ounces)	**Philadelphia ready-to-eat cheesecake filling**
1 can (21 ounces)	**pie filling,** any flavor
	whipped topping

Heat an electric griddle to 350 degrees. Prepare griddle with nonstick cooking spray.

In a 2-quart bowl, combine pancake mix and water. Batter will be slightly lumpy. Pour ¼ cup batter per pancake evenly onto hot griddle. Cook for 1–2 minutes on each side until golden brown.

Place a pancake each on 5 serving plates. Spread 2 tablespoons cheesecake filling over each pancake. Place another pancake over cheesecake filling. Spoon desired amount of pie filling over each pancake stack. Garnish with whipped topping. Makes 5 servings.

CITRUS-TOFFEE PANCAKES

2 cups	**pancake mix**
1 1/3 cups	**water**
1/4 cup	**orange marmalade**
1/3 cup	**Heath toffee bits**

Orange Syrup:

1 cup	**orange marmalade**
3 tablespoons	**orange juice**

Heat an electric griddle to 350 degrees. Prepare griddle with nonstick cooking spray.

In a 2-quart bowl, whisk together pancake mix, water, and 1/4 cup orange marmalade. Batter will be slightly lumpy. Stir in toffee bits. Pour 1/4 cup batter per pancake evenly onto hot griddle. Cook for 1−2 minutes on each side until golden brown.

Heat 1 cup orange marmalade and orange juice together in a 1-quart saucepan until marmalade is melted. Serve hot pancakes with warm syrup. Makes 14 pancakes.

NOTE: 1 jar (18 ounces) marmalade will yield enough for this recipe with a little left over for future use.

PEAR 'N RASPBERRY PANCAKES

Topping:

¹/₄ cup	**sugar**
¹/₂ cup	**water**
¹/₂ teaspoon	**nutmeg**
2 teaspoons	**butter or margarine**
1¹/₂ teaspoons	**lemon juice**
2 teaspoons	**cornstarch**
1 can (15.25 ounces)	**sliced pears,** drained and diced
¹/₂ cup	**raspberries**

Pancakes:

2 cups	**pancake mix**
1 teaspoon	**nutmeg**
1¹/₂ cups	**water**

For the topping; using a 1¹/₂-quart saucepan, combine sugar, water, nutmeg, butter, and lemon juice. Heat until butter melts. Slowly stir in cornstarch. Bring mixture to a boil. Boil for 1 minute. Stir in pears and cook until pears are heated. Stir in raspberries. Keep warm until ready to serve.

Heat an electric griddle to 350 degrees. Prepare griddle with nonstick cooking spray.

To make the pancakes; combine pancake mix and nutmeg in a 2-quart bowl. Whisk in water. Batter will be slightly lumpy. Pour ¹/₄ cup batter per pancake evenly onto hot griddle. Cook for 1–2 minutes on each side until golden brown. Serve hot pancakes with topping. Makes 12 pancakes.

PUMPKIN SPICE PANCAKES

2 1/3 cups	**pancake mix**
2 tablespoons	**sugar**
1 teaspoon	**pumpkin pie spice**
2	**eggs**
1 1/4 cups	**water**
1/2 cup	**canned pumpkin**
2 tablespoons	**olive or canola oil**

Nutmeg Whipped Topping:

1/2 container (8 ounces)	**whipped topping,** thawed
1 tablespoon	**sugar**
1/2 teaspoon	**vanilla**
1/2 teaspoon	**ground nutmeg**

Heat an electric griddle to 350 degrees. Prepare griddle with nonstick cooking spray.

In a 2-quart bowl, combine pancake mix, sugar and pumpkin pie spice. In a separate 1-quart bowl, beat together eggs, water, pumpkin, and oil until smooth. Whisk together the pancake mixture and the pumpkin mixture until moistened. Pour 1/4 cup batter per pancake evenly onto hot griddle. Cook for 1–2 minutes on each side until golden brown.

In a 1-quart bowl, combine whipped topping, sugar, vanilla, and nutmeg. Do not over mix. Serve hot pancakes topped with nutmeg whipped topping. Makes 17 pancakes.

RASPBERRY PANCAKES

Syrup:

I cup	**raspberries**
1/3 cup	**water**
3 tablespoons	**sugar**
I tablespoon	**cornstarch**
I teaspoon	**lemon juice**
2 cups	**pancake mix**
1 1/2 cups	**water**
I cup	**raspberries**
	Raspberry Syrup (see page 9)

For the syrup; using a 2-quart saucepan, combine raspberries and water. In a 1-quart bowl, combine sugar and cornstarch. Sprinkle sugar mixture over raspberries in pan. Stir in lemon juice. Cook over medium-high heat, stirring constantly, until syrup comes to a boil and thickens. Remove from heat. Cover and keep warm.

Heat an electric griddle to 350 degrees. Prepare griddle with nonstick cooking spray.

In a 2-quart bowl, whisk together pancake mix and water. Batter will be slightly lumpy. Fold in raspberries. Pour 1/4 cup batter per pancake evenly onto hot griddle. Cook for 1–2 minutes on each side until golden brown. Serve warm Raspberry Syrup over pancakes. Makes 14 pancakes.

OVEN-BAKED APPLE PANCAKE

¹/₄ cup	**butter or margarine**
2	**eggs**
1 cup	**milk**
¹/₂ teaspoon	**vanilla**
1¹/₂ cups	**pancake mix**
2	**small apples,** cored and thinly sliced
1 tablespoon	**cinnamon sugar**
	caramel sauce
	whipped cream

Preheat oven to 400 degrees.

While oven is heating, place butter in 9 x 13-inch pan and melt butter in oven. In a 2-quart bowl, beat eggs. Whisk in milk and vanilla. Mix in pancake mix.

Remove pan with melted butter from oven. Tilt pan to coat bottom of pan. Pour batter evenly over melted butter. Arrange apple slices over batter. Sprinkle apples with cinnamon sugar. Bake for 15–17 minutes until edges are golden brown. Cut and top individual servings with caramel sauce and whipped cream. Makes 12 servings.

AUTUMN CIDER PANCAKES

2 cups	**pancake mix**
1 tablespoon	**brown sugar**
2 teaspoons	**cinnamon**
1/2 teaspoon	**nutmeg**
1 1/2 cups	**apple cider or apple juice**
1/2 teaspoon	**vanilla**
	Maple Syrup (see page 7)

Heat an electric griddle to 350 degrees. Prepare griddle with nonstick cooking spray.

In a 2-quart bowl, combine pancake mix, brown sugar, cinnamon, and nutmeg. Whisk in apple cider and vanilla. Batter will be slightly lumpy. Pour 1/4 cup batter per pancake evenly onto hot griddle. Cook for 1–2 minutes on each side until golden brown. Top with hot Maple Syrup. Makes 12 pancakes.

CHOCOLATE CHIP PANCAKES

2 cups	**pancake mix**
1 1/2 cups	**water**
1/3 cup	**mini chocolate chips**
	sliced strawberries
	whipped topping
	chocolate syrup, optional

Heat an electric griddle to 350 degrees. Prepare griddle with nonstick cooking spray.

In a 2-quart bowl, whisk together pancake mix and water. Stir in chocolate chips. Batter will be slightly lumpy. Pour 1/4 cup batter per pancake evenly onto hot griddle. Cook for 1–2 minutes on each side until golden brown. Top individual pancakes with desired amounts of strawberries and whipped topping. Drizzle chocolate syrup over the top, if desired. Makes 12 pancakes.

CINNAMON AND SUGAR PANCAKE BITES

2 cups	**pancake mix**
2 tablespoons	**cinnamon sugar**
1 ½ cups	**vanilla-flavored soy milk**
1 teaspoon	**vanilla**
1 teaspoon	**honey**
	cinnamon sugar

Heat electric griddle to 350 degrees. Prepare griddle with nonstick cooking spray.

In a 2-quart bowl, combine pancake mix and cinnamon sugar. Whisk in milk. Stir in vanilla and honey. Using a 1 tablespoon-size cookie scoop, drop batter on a hot griddle. Cook for 1 minute on each side. Dip pancake bites in cinnamon and sugar. Makes 32 bites.

GRANOLA PANCAKES

2 cups	**pancake mix**
1 ½ cups	**water**
½ cup	**granola**
2 containers (6 ounces each)	**yogurt,** any flavor

Heat an electric griddle to 350 degrees. Prepare griddle with nonstick cooking spray.

In a 2-quart bowl, whisk together pancake mix and water. Stir in granola. Pour ¼ cup batter per pancake evenly onto hot griddle. Cook for 1–2 minutes on each side until golden brown. Serve pancakes topped with yogurt. Garnish with additional granola, if desired. Makes 12 pancakes.

OATMEAL PANCAKES

2 cups	**pancake mix**
1 cup	**quick oats**
2 tablespoons	**sugar**
1/2 tablespoon	**cinnamon**
2 cups	**water**
	Maple Syrup (see page 7),
	Coconut Syrup (see page 10), or
	Apple Syrup (see page 7)

Heat an electric griddle to 350 degrees. Prepare griddle with nonstick cooking spray.

In a 2-quart bowl, combine pancake mix, oats, sugar, and cinnamon. Whisk in water. Batter will be slightly lumpy. Pour 1/4 cup batter per pancake evenly onto hot griddle. Cook for 1–2 minutes on each side until golden brown. Serve with hot Maple Syrup, Coconut Syrup, or Apple Syrup. Makes 14 pancakes.

VARIATION: Stir in 1/2 cup raisins into batter before cooking.

JOHNNY CORN CAKES

I	**egg**
¹/₂ cup	**milk**
2 tablespoons	**canola or olive oil**
I ¹/₂ cups	**pancake mix**
I can (14.75 ounces)	**cream-style corn**
	applesauce or syrup of choice

Heat an electric griddle to 350 degrees. Prepare griddle with nonstick cooking spray.

In a 2-quart bowl, whisk together egg, milk, and oil until smooth. Stir in pancake mix and corn until combined. Pour ¹/₄ cup batter per pancake evenly onto hot griddle. Cook for 1–2 minutes on each side until golden brown. Serve with applesauce or syrup. Makes 13 pancakes.

KID FRIENDLY VERSION: Blend cream-style corn in the blender before adding it to the recipe.

PEANUT BUTTER PANCAKES

2 cups	**pancake mix**
2 tablespoons	**sugar**
2	**eggs**
²/₃ cup	**creamy peanut butter**
I can (12 ounces)	**evaporated milk**
¹/₂ cup	**water**
I teaspoon	**vanilla**
	peanut butter, to taste
	Maple Syrup (see page 7)

Heat an electric griddle to 350 degrees. Prepare griddle with nonstick cooking spray.

In a 2-quart bowl, combine pancake mix and sugar. In a 1-quart bowl, whisk together eggs and peanut butter. Gradually whisk in milk, water, and vanilla. Whisk the peanut butter mixture into the pancake mixture. Pour ¹/₄ cup batter per pancake evenly onto hot griddle. Cook for 1–2 minutes on each side until golden brown. Spread a thin layer of peanut butter over top of hot pancakes and drizzle with desired amount of Maple Syrup. Makes 18 pancakes.

POPPY SEED
YOGURT PANCAKES

1 container (6 ounces)	**vanilla or lemon yogurt**
1 cup	**water**
2 cups	**pancake mix**
1 tablespoon	**poppy seed**
$^1/_2$ tablespoon	**grated lemon peel**
2 teaspoons	**lemon juice**
	Coconut Syrup (see page 10)

Heat an electric griddle to 350 degrees. Prepare griddle with nonstick cooking spray.

In a 2-quart bowl, whisk together yogurt and water. Mix in pancake mix. Stir in poppy seed, lemon peel, and lemon juice. Pour $^1/_4$ cup batter per pancake evenly onto hot griddle. Cook for 1–2 minutes on each side until golden brown. Serve with Coconut Syrup. Makes 12 pancakes.

HIGH FIBER PANCAKES

2	**eggs**
2 1/4 cups	**milk,** divided
1 1/2 cups	**pancake mix**
3 cups	**crushed frosted Shredded Wheat cereal**
	syrup, of choice

Heat an electric griddle to 350 degrees. Prepare griddle with nonstick cooking spray.

In a 2-quart bowl, whisk together eggs and 1 1/2 cups milk. Whisk in pancake mix. Stir in crushed cereal. Let batter stand for 10 minutes. Batter will thicken as cereal softens. Stir in an additional 3/4 cup milk.

Pour 1/4 cup batter per pancake evenly onto hot griddle. Cook for 1–2 minutes on each side until golden brown. Serve with hot syrup. Makes 14 pancakes.

SOUR CREAM PANCAKES

1	**egg**
3/4 cup	**sour cream**
1/3 cup	**water**
1 tablespoon	**sugar**
1 cup	**pancake mix**
	dulce de leche, fruit jam,
	yogurt, or Maple Syrup
	(see page 7)

Heat an electric griddle to 350 degrees. Prepare griddle with nonstick cooking spray.

In a 2-quart bowl, beat egg. Whisk in sour cream and water until smooth. Add sugar. Mix in pancake mix. Batter will be slightly lumpy. Pour 1/4 cup batter per pancake evenly onto hot griddle. Cook for 1–2 minutes on each side until golden brown. Serve with dulce de leche, fruit jam, yogurt, or Maple Syrup. Makes 10 pancakes.

SIMPLE GINGERBREAD PANCAKES

2 cups	**wheat pancake mix**
1/4 cup	**molasses**
1 cup	**water**
2	**eggs**
1 tablespoon	**olive oil**
1 teaspoon	**cinnamon**
1/2 teaspoon	**nutmeg**
	Maple Syrup (see page 7)

Heat an electric griddle to 350 degrees. Prepare griddle with nonstick cooking spray.

In a 2-quart bowl, combine all ingredients until smooth. Pour 1/4 cup batter per pancake evenly onto hot griddle. Cook for 1–2 minutes on each side until golden brown. Serve with hot Maple Syrup. Makes 14 pancakes.

S'MORE PANCAKES

2 cups	**pancake mix**
1 1/2 cups	**water**
1 teaspoon	**vanilla**
1/3 cup	**graham cracker crumbs**
7 tablespoons	**marshmallow cream**
7 tablespoons	**milk chocolate chips**

Heat an electric griddle to 350 degrees. Prepare griddle with nonstick cooking spray.

In a 2-quart bowl, whisk together pancake mix, water, and vanilla. Drop less than 1/4 cup of batter per pancake evenly onto hot griddle. Sprinkle 1 teaspoon cracker crumbs over each uncooked pancake. Cook for 1–2 minutes on each side until golden brown.

Spread 1 tablespoon marshmallow cream over top of each pancake. Sprinkle 1 tablespoon chocolate chips over marshmallow. Top with another pancake. Garnish with additional graham cracker crumbs and chocolate chips, if desired. Makes 7 servings.

WAFFLES

APPLE CINNAMON WAFFLES

2 cups	**pancake mix**
I teaspoon	**cinnamon**
I ½ cups	**water**
2 tablespoons	**canola or olive oil**
½ cup	**peeled and diced apple**
	Apple Syrup (see page 7)

Heat waffle iron and prepare with nonstick cooking spray.

In a 2-quart bowl, combine pancake mix and cinnamon. Whisk in water and oil. Stir in apple. Pour ⅓ cup batter into each waffle space. Bake for 5 minutes or until steaming stops and waffles are golden brown. Carefully remove waffles. Serve syrup over hot waffles. Makes 8–9 waffles.

BANANA WALNUT WAFFLES

2 cups	**pancake mix**
I cup	**mashed banana***
I cup plus 2 tablespoons	**water**
2 tablespoons	**canola or olive oil**
$^{1}/_{4}$ cup	**chopped walnuts**
	caramel sauce, Maple Syrup
	(see page 7) or **Coconut Syrup**
	(see page 10)

Heat waffle iron and prepare with nonstick cooking spray.

In a 2-quart bowl, whisk together pancake mix, banana, water, and oil. Batter will be slightly lumpy. Fold in nuts. Pour $^{1}/_{3}$ cup batter into each waffle space. Bake for 5 minutes or until steaming stops and waffles are golden brown. Carefully remove waffles. Serve with warm caramel sauce, Maple Syrup or Coconut Syrup drizzled over top. Makes 10 waffles.

*2 medium bananas yield I cup mashed.

BLUEBERRY OAT WAFFLES

2 cups	**pancake mix**
1/2 cup	**quick oats**
3 tablespoons	**sugar**
1 1/2 cups	**water**
1	**egg**
2 tablespoons	**canola or olive oil**
1 cup	**blueberries**
	Blueberry Sauce (see page 10) or
	Mixed-Berry Syrup (see page 8)

Heat waffle iron and prepare with nonstick cooking spray.

In a 2-quart bowl, combine pancake mix, oats, and sugar. Mix in water, egg, and oil. Fold in blueberries. Pour 1/3 cup batter into each waffle space. Bake for 5 minutes or until steaming stops and waffles are golden brown. Carefully remove waffles. Serve topped with Blueberry Sauce or Mixed-Berry Syrup. Makes 10 waffles.

CHOCOLATE WAFFLES

2 cups	**pancake mix**
$1/2$ cup	**sugar**
$1/3$ cup	**unsweetened cocoa**
$1 1/2$ cups	**water**
2 tablespoons	**canola or olive oil**
	caramel sauce
	bananas, sliced

Heat waffle iron and prepare with nonstick cooking spray.

In a 2-quart bowl, combine pancake mix, sugar, and cocoa. Stir in water and oil. Batter will be slightly lumpy. Pour $1/3$ cup batter into each waffle space. Bake for 5 minutes or until steaming stops and waffles are golden brown. Carefully remove waffles. Serve topped with caramel sauce and bananas. Makes 12 waffles.

LEMON WAFFLES

2 cups	**pancake mix**
1 cup	**water**
2 tablespoons	**canola or olive oil**
1 container (6 ounces)	**lemon yogurt**
2 teaspoons	**grated lemon peel**

Lemon Cream:

$^1/_2$ pint	**whipping cream**
3 $^1/_2$ tablespoons	**powdered sugar**
1 teaspoon	**grated lemon peel**
$^1/_2$ package (8 ounces)	**cream cheese,** softened

Heat waffle iron and prepare with nonstick cooking spray.

In a 2-quart bowl, mix together pancake mix, water, and oil. Fold in yogurt and 2 teaspoons lemon peel. Pour $^1/_3$ cup batter into each waffle space. Bake for 5 minutes or until steaming stops and waffles are golden brown. Carefully remove waffles.

In a 2-quart bowl, mix together whipping cream, sugar, 1 teaspoon lemon peel, and cream cheese until soft peaks form. Chill until ready to serve. Serve hot waffles topped with lemon cream. Makes 9 waffles.

BANANA-PECAN BLENDER WAFFLES

1⅓ cups	**water**
2 tablespoons	**olive oil**
1	**egg**
¼ cup	**pecans**
1	**banana**
1 teaspoon	**cinnamon**
1 teaspoon	**honey**
1 teaspoon	**vanilla**
2 cups	**pancake mix**
	Maple Syrup (see page 7) or
	Coconut Syrup (see page 10)

Heat waffle iron and prepare with nonstick cooking spray.

In a blender, mix water, oil, egg, pecans, banana, cinnamon, honey, and vanilla. Add pancake mix ½ cup at a time and pulse blender in between until all of the pancake mix has been added. Pour ⅓ cup batter into each waffle space. Bake for 5 minutes or until steaming stops and waffles are golden brown. Carefully remove waffles. Serve with Maple Syrup or Coconut Syrup. Makes 11 waffles.

PEACHES-AND-CREAM WAFFLES

3 cups	**pancake mix**
2 tablespoons	**sugar**
2 cups	**water**
2 tablespoons	**canola or olive oil**
I can (15 ounces)	**sliced peaches,** drained and diced

Cream:

1/2 pint	**whipping cream**
3 1/2 tablespoons	**powdered sugar**
1/2 package (8 ounces)	**cream cheese,** softened

Heat waffle iron and prepare with nonstick cooking spray.

In a 2-quart bowl, mix together pancake mix, sugar, water, and oil. Fold in diced peaches. Pour 1/3 cup batter into each waffle space. Bake for 5 minutes or until steaming stops and waffles are golden brown. Carefully remove waffles.

In a 2-quart bowl, mix together whipping cream, sugar, and cream cheese until soft peaks form. Chill until ready to serve. Serve hot waffles topped with cream. Makes 14 waffles.

RASPBERRY
YOGURT WAFFLES

2 cups	**pancake mix**
1 cup	**water**
2 tablespoons	**canola or olive oil**
1 container (6 ounces)	**raspberry yogurt**
	Mixed-Berry Syrup (see page 8)

Heat waffle iron and prepare with nonstick cooking spray.

In a 2-quart bowl, whisk together all ingredients. Batter will be slightly lumpy. Pour 1/3 cup batter into each waffle space. Bake for 5 minutes or until steaming stops and waffles are golden brown. Carefully remove waffles. Top with Mixed-Berry Syrup. Makes 12 waffles.

SOUR CREAM WAFFLES

1 cup	**milk**
1 cup	**sour cream**
1	**egg**
¼ cup	**canola or olive oil**
3 tablespoons	**sugar**
2 cups	**pancake mix**

Heat waffle iron and prepare with nonstick cooking spray.

In a 2-quart bowl, whisk together milk, sour cream, egg, oil, and sugar until smooth. Whisk in pancake mix. Batter will be slightly lumpy. Pour ⅓ cup batter into each waffle space. Bake for 5 minutes or until steaming stops and waffles are golden brown. Carefully remove waffles. Makes 12 waffles.

VARIATION: Fold in ½ cup fresh or frozen raspberries or blueberries. Top waffles with vanilla yogurt and additional berries.

POPPY SEED WAFFLES

2 cups	**pancake mix**
I tablespoon	**sugar**
I tablespoon	**poppy seeds**
I tablespoon	**grated lemon peel**
I ½ cups	**water**
2 tablespoons	**canola or olive oil**
2 containers (6 ounces each)	**vanilla yogurt**
	fresh berries, if desired

Heat waffle iron and prepare with nonstick cooking spray.

In a 2-quart bowl, combine pancake mix, sugar, poppy seeds, and lemon peel. Whisk in water and oil. Batter will be slightly lumpy. Pour ⅓ cup batter into each waffle space. Bake for 5 minutes or until steaming stops and waffles are golden brown. Carefully remove waffles. Spoon yogurt and fresh berries over individual waffles. Makes 8–9 waffles.

RICOTTA WAFFLES

2 ½ cups	**pancake mix**
2 ½ cups	**milk**
I container (15 ounces)	**ricotta cheese**
2 tablespoons	**olive or canola oil**

Heat waffle iron and prepare with nonstick cooking spray.

In a 2-quart bowl, whisk together pancake mix, milk, cheese, and oil. Pour ⅓ cup batter into each waffle space. Bake for 5 minutes or until steaming stops and waffles are golden brown. Carefully remove waffles. Top with favorite waffle toppings or syrup. Makes 15 waffles.

GRANOLA WHEAT WAFFLES

2 cups	**wheat pancake mix**
$1/2$ cup	**granola**
1 $1/4$ cups	**water**
2 tablespoons	**olive or canola oil**
1 container (6 ounces)	**vanilla yogurt**

Heat waffle iron and prepare with nonstick cooking spray.

In a 2-quart bowl, combine pancake mix and granola. Stir in water, oil, and yogurt until blended. Pour $1/3$ cup batter into each waffle space. Bake for 5 minutes or until steaming stops and waffles are golden brown. Carefully remove waffles. Serve with your favorite syrup. Makes 8–9 waffles.

OTHER
BREAKFAST
SENSATIONS

INSTANT CINNAMON ROLLS

4 1/2 cups	**pancake mix**
1 1/3 cups	**milk**
1/4 cup	**butter or margarine,** softened
1/2 cup	**brown sugar**
1 1/2 teaspoons	**cinnamon**
1 container (16 ounces)	**cream cheese frosting**

Preheat oven to 450 degrees.

In a 3-quart bowl, combine pancake mix and milk. If using a stand mixer, mix with bread hook for 2–3 minutes until dough is thoroughly formed. If making dough by hand, knead 8–10 times. Roll the dough into a 10 x 14-inch rectangle on a lightly floured or nonstick surface.

In a small microwaveable bowl, combine the butter, sugar and cinnamon. Microwave for 10 seconds, stir again, and spread mixture over dough. Roll up dough into a log starting with the long side.

Use dental floss to slice roll into 16 pieces. Place slices on a baking sheet prepared with nonstick cooking spray. Bake for 10–12 minutes until golden brown. While still warm, frost rolls with desired amount of frosting. Makes 16 rolls.

PINEAPPLE-FILLED DONUTS

	vegetable or canola oil
1 can (20 ounces)	**pineapple slices,** drained
1 cup	**pancake mix**
3/4 cup	**water**
1 teaspoon	**vanilla**
	powdered sugar

Heat oil in deep fryer or 4-quart saucepan to 375 degrees.

Lay pineapple slices on a platter lined with paper towels to soak up
any excess juice. In a shallow bowl, whisk together pancake mix,
water, and vanilla. Batter will be slightly lumpy. Coat pineapple slices
in batter. Fry in hot oil for 1–2 minutes on each side until golden
brown. Place donuts on another plate covered in paper towels to drain.
Sprinkle powdered sugar over donuts. Makes 10 donuts.

GRAHAM CRACKER PANCAKE PUFFS

	vegetable or canola oil
2 cups	**pancake mix**
¹/₂ tablespoon	**cinnamon**
1 cup	**milk**
1 teaspoon	**vanilla**
2 tablespoons	**butter or margarine,** melted
1 cup	**graham cracker crumbs**
	powdered sugar or
	cinnamon and sugar

Heat oil in deep fryer or 4-quart saucepan to 375 degrees.

In a 2-quart bowl, combine pancake mix and cinnamon. Add milk and vanilla, stirring until combined. In a separate 1-quart bowl, combine butter and cracker crumbs until crumbs are coated with butter. Stir crumb mixture into pancake mixture.

Using a 2 tablespoon-size cookie scoop, drop balls of dough into deep fryer. Fry in hot oil for 1–2 minutes on each side until golden brown. Place cooked puffs on a plate covered in paper towels. Roll puffs in powdered sugar or cinnamon and sugar. Makes 18 puffs.

ARTICHOKE ONION FRITTATA

3 tablespoons	**olive oil**
1	**large onion,** chopped
1 jar (14.75 ounces)	**marinated artichoke hearts,** drained and chopped
1/2 cup	**water**
6	**eggs**
1/2 cup	**pancake mix**
1 teaspoon	**salt**
1/2 teaspoon	**pepper**
3/4 cup	**grated colby and Monterey Jack cheese mix,** divided

Preheat oven to 325 degrees.

Heat oil in a large frying pan. Stir in onion and saute for 2 minutes. Stir in artichokes and water. Saute for an additional 2 minutes. Remove from heat.

In a 2-quart bowl, beat eggs until smooth. Beat in pancake mix, salt, and pepper. Stir in onion mixture and 1/2 cup cheese. Pour into a 9-inch deep dish pie pan that has been prepared with nonstick cooking spray. Bake for 25–30 minutes or until center is firm. Sprinkle remaining cheese over top. Makes 6–8 servings.

SAUSAGE-MUSHROOM BREAKFAST BAKE

1 pound	**ground sausage,** browned, crumbled, and drained
¹/₂ cup	**chopped green onions**
1 can (4 ounces)	**mushroom pieces,** drained
2	**medium tomatoes,** seeded and diced
1 ¹/₂ cups	**grated cheddar cheese**
12	**eggs**
1 cup	**pancake mix**
1 teaspoon	**Italian seasoning**
¹/₂ teaspoon	**salt**
¹/₄ teaspoon	**pepper**

Preheat oven to 350 degrees.

Prepare a 9 x 13-inch pan with nonstick cooking spray. Layer sausage, onions, mushrooms, tomatoes, and cheese evenly in the pan.

In a blender, mix together eggs, pancake mix, seasoning, salt, and pepper. Pour egg mixture evenly over layered ingredients. Bake, uncovered, for 45–50 minutes until the center is set and the top is golden brown. Cool for 5–10 minutes before serving. Makes 12 servings.

APPLE COFFEE CAKE

2 1/2 cups	**pancake mix**
1/2 cup	**sugar**
1 teaspoon	**cinnamon**
1/2 teaspoon	**nutmeg**
3/4 cup	**water**
1	**egg**
2 tablespoons	**canola or olive oil**
1 teaspoon	**vanilla**
1 1/2 cups	**peeled and diced apple**

Topping:

3/4 cup	**chopped pecans**
2/3 cup	**pancake mix**
1/4 cup	**brown sugar**
1 teaspoon	**cinnamon**
3 tablespoons	**butter or margarine,** melted

Preheat oven to 350 degrees.

In a 2-quart bowl, combine pancake mix, sugar, cinnamon, and nutmeg. Whisk in water, egg, oil, and vanilla. With a rubber spatula, fold in apples. Spread batter into a 9 x 9-inch pan prepared with nonstick cooking spray.

In a 1-quart bowl, combine pecans, pancake mix, brown sugar, and cinnamon. Add butter and mix until crumbly. Sprinkle topping over batter. Bake for 28–33 minutes. Serve warm. Makes 9 servings.

COCONUT-PECAN COFFEE CAKE

Topping:

2 tablespoons	**butter or margarine**
1/3 cup	**brown sugar**
2/3 cup	**sweetened coconut flakes**
1/2 cup	**chopped pecans**
1/3 cup	**pancake syrup**

Cake:

2	**eggs**
1/2 cup	**brown sugar**
1/2 cup	**milk**
2 tablespoons	**canola or olive oil**
1 teaspoon	**cinnamon**
1 teaspoon	**vanilla**
2 cups	**pancake mix**

Preheat oven to 400 degrees.

Place butter in a 9 x 9-inch pan and place pan in the oven. Once the butter melts, remove pan from oven. Move pan around until butter evenly coats the bottom. In a 1-quart bowl, combine 1/3 cup brown sugar, coconut, pecans, and syrup. Evenly spoon the mixture over the hot butter. Let mixture sit for one minute to soften then spread evenly over the bottom.

In a 2-quart bowl, whisk eggs until smooth. Add brown sugar, milk, oil, cinnamon and vanilla. Whisk until smooth. Whisk in pancake mix. Batter will be slightly lumpy. Pour batter evenly over top of coconut-pecan layer. Use a rubber spatula to smooth out the top. Bake for 18–22 minutes until golden brown. Remove cake from the oven and while hot, invert onto a square platter. Spoon any remaining pecan mixture from pan evenly over the cake. Let stand for 5 minutes or longer before serving. Makes 9 servings.

DUTCH BABY CAKES

¹/₂ cup	**milk**
¹/₂ cup	**pancake mix**
3	**eggs**
2 tablespoons	**butter or margarine,** melted
pinch of	**salt**
¹/₂ pound	**strawberries**
I tablespoon	**sugar**
	powdered sugar
	whipped cream

Preheat oven to 400 degrees.

Prepare a 12-cup muffin pan with nonstick cooking spray. Blend milk, pancake mix, eggs, butter, and salt in blender. Fill each muffin cup about ¹/₄ full. Distribute any remaining batter evenly over cups. Bake for 15 minutes. While baking, they will puff up like muffins. Once removed from the oven, they will flatten.

Wash and hull strawberries and cut into small chunks. Place berries in a I-quart bowl. Sprinkle with sugar. Stir to coat and let stand until ready to use.

When done baking, immediately remove the cakes from the pan and place them on a platter. Sprinkle powdered sugar evenly over top. Place 3 cakes on a plate. Top each with strawberries and whipped cream. Repeat for 3 more plates. Makes 4 servings.

STRAWBERRY CREPES

1 pound	**strawberries**
1 tablespoon	**sugar**
3	**eggs**
2 tablespoons	**olive or canola oil**
1 cup	**water**
¾ cup	**pancake mix**
1 container (8 ounces)	**whipped topping,** thawed
	powdered sugar

Wash, hull, and slice strawberries. Place berries in a 1-quart bowl and sprinkle sugar evenly over slices. Carefully fold in sugar to coat. Allow to stand while you make the crepes.

In a 2-quart bowl, beat eggs until smooth. Whisk in oil and water. Slowly mix in pancake mix until fairly smooth. Let batter stand for 5 minutes while you heat a 6- to 7-inch frying pan over medium-high heat. Prepare hot pan with nonstick cooking spray. Pour ⅛ cup batter into hot pan. Immediately tilt the pan to evenly coat the bottom of the pan with batter. Return to the burner. Cook for 30–60 seconds until top appears dry. Flip crepe and cook an additional 30 seconds. Continue with the remaining batter.

Place strawberries and whipped cream in center of crepes. Wrap crepes around the filling and dust with the powdered sugar to serve. Makes 18 crepes.

PEACHES-AND-CREAM CREPES

3	**eggs**
2 tablespoons	**olive or canola oil**
I cup	**water**
¾ cup	**pancake mix**
	vanilla frozen yogurt
I pound	**peaches,** peeled and diced
	powdered sugar

In a 2-quart bowl, beat eggs until smooth. Whisk in oil and water.
Slowly mix in pancake mix until fairly smooth. Let batter stand for
5 minutes while you heat a 6- to 7-inch frying pan over medium-high
heat. Prepare hot pan with nonstick cooking spray. Pour $\frac{1}{8}$ cup batter
into hot pan. Immediately tilt the pan to evenly coat the bottom of the
pan with batter. Return to the burner. Cook for 30–60 seconds until
top appears dry. Flip crepe and cook an additional 30 seconds.

Place frozen yogurt and peaches in center of crepes. Wrap crepes
around the filling and dust with the powdered sugar to serve. Makes
18 crepes.

NOTE: Vanilla or peach yogurt can be used in place of frozen yogurt.

CINNAMON-APPLE BREAKFAST SQUARES

1/3 cup	**butter or margarine**
2	**apples,** cored, peeled and thinly sliced
6	**eggs**
1 1/2 cups	**milk**
1 cup	**pancake mix**
3 tablespoons	**sugar**
1 teaspoon	**vanilla**
1 teaspoon	**cinnamon**
1/4 teaspoon	**salt**
2 tablespoons	**brown sugar**
	Maple Syrup (see page 7) or **Apple Syrup** (see page 7)

Preheat oven to 425 degrees.

Place butter in a 9 x 13-inch glass or stone pan and place pan in the oven until butter melts. Move butter around pan to evenly coat the bottom. Lay apple slices evenly over butter. Place pan back in oven and bake for 8–10 minutes until butter is sizzling.

In a blender, mix together the eggs, milk, pancake mix, sugar, vanilla, cinnamon, and salt. Pour evenly over apples. Sprinkle brown sugar evenly over the top. Bake for 20 minutes or until golden brown. Cut into 12 squares. Serve immediately with Maple Syrup or Apple Syrup drizzled over top. Makes 12 servings.

STRAWBERRY BREAKFAST CAKE

¹/₄ cup	**butter or margarine,** melted
4 tablespoons	**sugar,** divided
2 cups	**sliced strawberries**
2	**eggs**
I cup	**milk**
2 cups	**pancake mix**
I teaspoon	**vanilla**

Preheat oven to 350 degrees.

Pour melted butter into a 9 x 9-inch pan. Using a pastry brush, brush butter up the sides and over the bottom of pan. Sprinkle 2 tablespoons sugar evenly over the butter in the bottom of pan.

Evenly place strawberries over bottom of pan.

In a 2-quart bowl, whisk together eggs and milk until smooth. Whisk in remaining 2 tablespoons sugar, pancake mix, and vanilla. Batter will be slightly lumpy. Pour batter evenly over strawberry layer. Bake for 30–35 minutes until golden brown. Immediately run a knife around the edges of cake and invert onto a square platter. Serve warm. Makes 9 servings.

YUMMY EGGY PANCAKE BAKE

¹/₄ cup	**butter or margarine**
I cup	**milk**
I cup	**pancake mix**
6	**eggs**
dash	**salt**
	powdered sugar
	Coconut Syrup (see page 10) or
	Maple Syrup (see page 7)

Preheat oven to 400 degrees.

Place butter in a 9 x 13-inch glass or stone pan and place pan in the oven until butter melts. Move butter around pan to evenly coat the bottom.

In a blender, mix together the milk, pancake mix, eggs, and salt. Pour batter evenly over melted butter. Bake for 20–25 minutes. Sprinkle powdered sugar over the top. Cut into 12 squares. Serve with Coconut Syrup or Maple Syrup. Makes 6 servings.

ZUCCHINI BREAKFAST BAKE

4	**eggs**
3 cups	**diced zucchini**
I	**onion,** chopped
I cup	**pancake mix**
$^{1}/_{2}$ cup	**canola or olive oil**
$^{1}/_{2}$ cup	**grated Parmesan cheese**
$^{1}/_{2}$ teaspoon	**Italian seasoning**
pinch of	**pepper**

Preheat oven to 350 degrees. In a 2-quart bowl, beat eggs until smooth. Stir in zucchini, onion, pancake mix, oil, cheese, seasoning, and pepper. Spread mixture into a 6 x 10-inch pan prepared with nonstick cooking spray. Bake for 30 minutes or until golden brown. Makes 6 servings.

DINNER DISHES

RANCH SEASONED CHICKEN

1 envelope (1.125 ounces)	**ranch dressing mix**
1/3 cup	**pancake mix**
1	**egg**
1/4 cup	**water**
4	**skinless, boneless chicken breast halves**

Preheat oven to 375 degrees.

Combine dressing mix and pancake mix in a gallon-size ziplock bag. In a 1-quart bowl, whisk together egg and water until smooth. Prepare a baking sheet with nonstick cooking spray. Dip a chicken breast in egg mixture and then place in ziplock bag. Seal and shake to coat. Lay coated chicken on baking sheet. Repeat the process for the remaining chicken breasts. Bake for 25–30 minutes, or until chicken is done. Makes 4 servings.

BAKED ITALIAN-CRUSTED CHICKEN

1 ½ cups	**pancake mix**
1 envelope (.7 ounce)	**Italian dressing mix**
1 tablespoon	**dried oregano**
2 teaspoons	**dried basil**
3 pounds	**skinless, boneless chicken breast halves**
½ cup	**olive oil**

Preheat oven to 400 degrees.

Combine pancake mix, dressing mix, oregano, and basil in a gallon-size ziplock bag. Cut chicken breasts in half. Dip pieces in oil and place 2 pieces at a time in the bag. Seal and shake to coat chicken. Place coated chicken on a baking sheet prepared with nonstick cooking spray. Repeat for remaining chicken. Bake for 25–30 minutes until done. Makes 6–8 servings.

COCONUT BATTERED SHRIMP

	vegetable or canola oil
¾ cup	**pancake mix**
¾ cup	**apple juice**
¼ cup	**flour**
I cup	**flaked coconut**
½ pound	**medium raw shrimp,** peeled and deveined

Heat oil in deep fryer or 4-quart saucepan to 350 degrees.

In a 2-quart bowl, whisk together pancake mix and apple juice. Place flour and coconut into separate small bowls.

Dip shrimp in flour and shake off any excess. Dip shrimp in pancake batter and immediately into coconut. Fry for 45–60 seconds on each side until golden. Place fried shrimp on a plate covered in paper towels to drain. Makes 4 servings.

BISCUIT TOPPED STROGANOFF

1 ½ pounds	**steak,** cut into bite-size pieces
1 cup	**chopped onion**
2 tablespoons	**flour**
1 ½ cups	**water**
1 teaspoon	**salt**
1 teaspoon	**Worcestershire sauce**
½ teaspoon	**pepper**
1 can (10.5 ounces)	**cream of mushroom soup,** condensed
½ cup	**sour cream**

Biscuits:

½ cup	**sour cream**
1 cup	**pancake mix**
1	**egg**
2 teaspoons	**dried parsley**
2 teaspoons	**sesame seeds**
½ teaspoons	**dried basil**

Preheat oven to 350 degrees.

Brown pieces of steak in a large frying pan over medium-high heat. Drain any excess fat. Add the onion and saute for 4 minutes or until tender. Stir in flour. Slowly stir in water ½ cup at a time. Reduce heat to low. Stir in salt, Worcestershire sauce, pepper, and soup until sauce is smooth. Stir in ½ cup sour cream. Leave on low heat.

In a 2-quart bowl, combine all biscuit ingredients. Pour stroganoff mixture into a 9 x 9-inch pan prepared with nonstick cooking spray. Drop tablespoonfuls of dough evenly over top of stroganoff. Bake for 25 minutes or until bubbly and biscuits are a light golden brown. Makes 6 servings.

INSTANT CHICKEN POT PIE

1 can (12.5 ounces)	**cooked chicken breast,** drained
1 can (29 ounces)	**Veg-All mixed vegetables,** drained
2 cans (10.5 ounces each)	**cream of celery or cream of potato soup,** condensed
1/2 teaspoon	**garlic**
1 cup	**pancake mix**
1/2 cup	**milk**
1	**egg**
1/2 teaspoon	**Italian seasoning**

Preheat oven to 400 degrees.

In a 2-quart bowl, break chicken into bite-size pieces. Stir in vegetables, soup, and garlic. Spread vegetable mixture into a 9 x 9-inch pan prepared with nonstick cooking spray.

In a 1-quart bowl, whisk together pancake mix, milk, egg, and seasoning. Batter will be slightly lumpy. Spread batter mixture over top of chicken. Bake for 30 minutes until golden brown. Makes 6–8 servings.

VARIATION: Sprinkle 1 1/4 cups grated cheddar cheese over chicken mixture and then spread pancake mixture over top.

CHEESEBURGER CASSEROLE

1 pound	**lean ground beef**
1	**large onion,** chopped
1/2 tablespoon	**cumin**
1/2 teaspoon	**salt**
1 cup	**grated cheddar cheese**
1/2 cup	**pancake mix**
1 cup	**milk**
2	**eggs**
	fresh salsa

Preheat oven to 400 degrees.

In a large frying pan, brown ground beef and onion together until meat is crumbly and thoroughly cooked. Drain, if necessary. Stir in cumin and salt. Spread the meat mixture evenly over the bottom of an 8 x 8-inch pan prepared with nonstick cooking spray. Sprinkle cheese over meat.

In a 2-quart bowl, whisk together pancake mix, milk, and eggs until only small lumps remain. Pour batter evenly over meat and cheese. Bake for 25 minutes or until center is set. Serve with salsa spooned over top of each serving. Makes 6–8 servings.

BREADED TILAPIA STICKS

	vegetable or canola oil
I pound	**boneless and skinless tilapia**
$^1/_2$ cup	**pancake mix**
$^1/_2$ cup	**Italian breadcrumbs**
$^1/_4$ teaspoon	**garlic power**
$^1/_4$ teaspoon	**lemon pepper**
$^1/_4$ teaspoon	**salt**
I	**egg**
$^1/_4$ cup	**water**
	tartar sauce

Heat oil in deep fryer or 4-quart saucepan to 350 degrees.

Cut fish into sticks. In a gallon-size ziplock bag, add pancake mix, breadcrumbs, garlic, lemon pepper, and salt. Shake to combine. In a I-quart bowl, whisk together egg and water. Dip fish sticks in egg mixture and drop into breadcrumb mixture and shake to coat. Place fish in hot oil and fry for 5–7 minutes, until golden brown. Serve hot with tartar sauce. Makes 4–6 servings.

COUNTRY-STYLE PIZZA

1 ¾ cups	**pancake mix**
⅓ cup	**grated Parmesan cheese**
¼ cup	**milk**
2 tablespoons	**canola or olive oil**
1	**egg**
1 can (8 ounces)	**tomato sauce**
1 teaspoon	**Italian seasoning**
¼ teaspoon	**salt**
½ package (6 ounces)	**sliced Canadian bacon**
¼ cup	**chopped onion**
⅓ cup	**chopped green bell pepper**
1 cup	**grated mozzarella cheese**

Preheat oven to 450 degrees.

Prepare a 14-inch pizza pan with nonstick cooking spray. In a 2-quart bowl, combine pancake mix and Parmesan cheese. Stir in milk, oil, and egg until dough forms. Spread dough over pan. Bake for 5–8 minutes. Remove from oven.

In a 1-quart bowl, combine tomato sauce, seasoning, and salt. Spread sauce over crust. Distribute bacon evenly over sauce. Sprinkle onion and bell pepper over top followed by cheese. Bake for 8–10 minutes until cheese melts. Makes 4–6 servings.

SOUTHWEST CHILI CASSEROLE

1	**egg**
2 cans (15 ounces each)	**chili,** any variety
1 can (11 ounces)	**Mexicorn,** drained
1/2 cup	**grated Monterey Jack cheese**

Topping:

1 cup	**milk**
2	**eggs**
2 1/2 cups	**pancake mix**
1/2 teaspoon	**garlic salt**
3/4 cup	**grated Monterey Jack cheese**

Preheat oven to 375 degrees.

In a 2-quart bowl, beat egg. Stir in chili, corn, and 1/2 cup cheese. Spread chili mixture into a 9 x 13-inch pan prepared with nonstick cooking spray.

In a 2-quart bowl, whisk together milk and eggs until smooth. Stir in pancake mix and salt. Spoon dough evenly over chili mixture. Bake uncovered for 25–30 minutes until golden brown. Sprinkle remaining cheese over top. Bake an additional 5 minutes until cheese melts. Makes 8–10 servings.

LEMON PEPPER
CRUSTED PERCH

2 $\frac{1}{2}$ cups	**lemon-lime soda**
1 pound	**perch fillets**
1 $\frac{1}{2}$ cups	**pancake mix**
1 tablespoon	**lemon pepper**
	vegetable or canola oil

Pour soda into a shallow dish just big enough to hold fish fillets. Place fillets in soda and let soak for 15–30 minutes. Soda should cover fish.

In a shallow bowl, combine pancake mix and pepper. Dip both sides of fillets into pancake mix. Heat $\frac{1}{4}$-inch oil in a large frying pan over medium-high heat. Brown fish for 2–3 minutes on each side in hot oil. Fish will flake with a fork when done. Place on a plate covered with paper towels to drain. Makes 3–4 servings.

P.B. AND BANANA PANWICHES

2 cups	**pancake mix**
1½ cups	**water**
6 tablespoons	**peanut butter**
2	**bananas,** sliced

Heat an electric griddle to 350 degrees and prepare with nonstick cooking spray.

In a 2-quart bowl, combine pancake mix and water. Pour ¼ cup batter per pancake evenly onto hot griddle. Cook for 1–2 minutes on each side until golden brown. Spread peanut butter and banana slices over 6 of the pancakes and top with another pancake. Makes 6 panwiches.

VARIATIONS: You can use peanut butter and jam, peanut butter and honey, or cream cheese and sliced strawberries instead of peanut butter and bananas.

POTATO PANCAKES

5 pounds	**russet potatoes,** peeled
1	**medium onion**
3	**eggs**
2½ cups	**pancake mix**
1 tablespoon	**minced garlic**
2 teaspoons	**salt**
1 teaspoon	**pepper**
	canola or olive oil

Using a food processor, grate potatoes and onion. Do not drain water. In a 3-quart bowl, beat eggs. Stir in potatoes and onion. Add pancake mix, garlic, salt, and pepper. Stir until well blended. Heat 1 tablespoon oil in a large frying pan. Spoon a 3 tablespoon-size portion of potato mixture into hot frying pan. Fry 3–4 minutes on each side. Add more oil as needed to fry remaining potato mixture. Makes 15 servings.

SWEET CRABBY CAKES

3 tablespoons	**pancake mix**
I tablespoon	**prepared yellow mustard**
3 tablespoons	**mayonnaise**
I	**egg**
I teaspoon	**dried parsley**
I pound	**cooked and flaked crab meat**
2½ to 3 cups	**vegetable oil**

In a 2-quart bowl, mix together pancake mix, mustard, mayonnaise, and egg. Fold in parsley and crab. Form into 7 patties (approximately 3 tablespoons each). Heat oil in a large frying pan. Oil should reach halfway up crab cakes while they cook. Carefully place patties in hot oil. Fry about 8 minutes on each side until golden brown. Place fried cakes on a platter lined with paper towels to drain. Makes 7 cakes.

ZUCCHINI GARDEN PANCAKES

1 ½ cups	**pancake mix**
¼ cup	**cornmeal**
2 teaspoons	**sugar**
¼ teaspoon	**salt**
1 pinch	**pepper**
1 cup	**water**
1	**small zucchini,** coarsely shredded
½ cup	**frozen corn,** thawed
1 container (6 ounces)	**plain yogurt**
2	**medium tomatoes,** seeded and diced
⅓ cup	**chopped fresh cilantro**

Heat an electric griddle to 350 degrees and prepare with nonstick cooking spray.

In a 2-quart bowl, combine pancake mix, cornmeal, sugar, salt, and pepper. Stir in water and zucchini. Batter will be slightly lumpy. Fold in corn. Pour ¼ cup batter per pancake evenly onto hot griddle. Cook each pancake for 1–2 minutes on each side until golden brown. Top individual cakes with yogurt, tomatoes, and cilantro. Makes 10 pancakes.

DESSERTS

STRAWBERRY SHORTCAKE

4 cups	**sliced strawberries**
¼ cup plus 3 tablespoons	**sugar,** divided
2 cups	**pancake mix**
½ cup	**milk**
3 tablespoons	**butter or margarine,** melted
I container (8 ounces)	**frozen whipped topping,** thawed

Heat oven to 425 degrees.

In a 2-quart bowl, combine strawberries and ¼ cup sugar. Set aside.

In another 2-quart bowl, combine pancake mix, milk, remaining sugar, and butter. Divide dough into 8 portions and place onto an ungreased baking sheet. Bake for I0–I2 minutes until golden brown.

Split warm shortcakes. Spoon strawberries and topping over bottom layers. Replace tops and garnish with more topping and berries. Makes 8 servings.

VARIATION: Spoon 2 tablespoons Philadelphia ready-to-eat cheesecake filling over shortcake bottom layer. Spoon strawberries over top. Place shortcake top over cheesecake filling and strawberries. Spoon more strawberries over top and garnish with whipped cream.

EASY CHOCOLATE PIE

Crust:

1 ½ cups	**pancake mix**
1 tablespoon	**sugar**
4 tablespoons	**butter or margarine**
2 tablespoons	**olive or canola oil**
2 tablespoons	**water**

Filling:

1 box (5.9 ounces)	**instant chocolate pudding mix**
2 cups	**milk**
½ container (8 ounces)	**frozen whipped topping,** thawed
2 to 3 tablespoons	**mini chocolate chips**

Preheat oven to 350 degrees.

In a 2-quart bowl, combine pancake mix and sugar. Using a pastry blender, blend butter into pancake mixture until butter is completely worked into the mixture. Stir in oil and water until dough forms. Spread dough into a 9-inch pie pan prepared with nonstick cooking spray. Bake for 15 minutes until lightly golden. Allow crust to completely cool.

In a 2-quart bowl, whisk together pudding mix and milk until smooth and thickened. Immediately pour chocolate pudding into the cooled crust. Chill for 10–15 minutes. Spread topping over pie and sprinkle with chocolate chips. Makes 8 servings.

BANANA CREAM DELIGHT

2 cups	**pancake mix**
2 tablespoons	**sugar**
½ cup	**butter or margarine**
1 box (5.1 ounces)	**instant banana pudding mix**
2¾ cups	**milk**
2	**bananas,** sliced
1 container (8 ounces)	**frozen whipped topping,** thawed

Preheat oven to 375 degrees.

In a 2-quart bowl, combine pancake mix and sugar. Use a pastry blender to cut butter into the pancake mixture until crumbly. Press over the bottom of a 9 x 9-inch pan prepared with nonstick cooking spray. Bake for 15 minutes until light brown around the edges. Allow crust to cool completely.

In a 1-quart bowl, whisk together pudding mix and milk until pudding starts to thicken. Spread ½ pudding mixture evenly over cooled crust. Lay sliced bananas evenly over pudding layer. Top with remaining pudding. Spread desired amount of whipped topping evenly over pudding layer. Makes 9 servings.

ICED SUGAR COOKIES

¹/₂ cup	**butter or margarine,** softened
I cup	**sugar**
2	**eggs**
I teaspoon	**vanilla extract**
2³/₄ cups	**pancake mix**

Icing:

2 cups	**powdered sugar**
2 tablespoons	**milk**
4 teaspoons	**light corn syrup**
¹/₂ teaspoon	**vanilla or almond extract**
	assorted food coloring

In a 2-quart bowl, cream together butter and sugar until smooth. Mix in eggs, one at a time. Stir in vanilla. Stir in pancake mix until dough forms. Chill for 30 minutes.

Preheat oven to 350 degrees. Roll dough onto a nonstick or lightly floured surface until the dough is ¹/₄-inch thick. Use cookie cutters to cut dough into desired shapes. Place on a baking sheet prepared with nonstick cooking spray. Bake for 12–15 minutes. Allow cookies to cool.

In a I-quart bowl, stir together powdered sugar and milk. Mix in corn syrup and extract until smooth. Divide icing into separate bowls. Add food coloring until each reaches the desired color. Ice tops of cookies with the icing of choice. Makes 16 cookies.

BUTTERSCOTCH-CHOCOLATE CHIP CRUNCH COOKIES

½ cup	**butter or margarine,** softened
½ cup	**sugar**
1	**egg**
1 teaspoon	**almond extract**
1 ¼ cups	**wheat and honey pancake mix**
⅓ cup	**butterscotch chips**
⅓ cup	**chocolate chips**
1 cup	**crispy rice cereal**

Preheat oven to 350 degrees.

In a 2-quart bowl, cream butter and sugar together. Mix in egg and extract. Stir in pancake mix. Stir in chips and cereal. Using a 1 tablespoon-size cookie scoop, drop dough onto a baking sheet prepared with nonstick cooking spray. Bake for 10–12 minutes. Makes 24 cookies.

DECADENT
PEANUT BUTTER COOKIES

1 can (14 ounces)	**sweetened condensed milk**
3/4 cup	**creamy peanut butter**
1	**egg**
1 teaspoon	**vanilla**
2 cups	**pancake mix**
1/3 cup	**sugar**

In a 3-quart bowl, mix together milk, peanut butter, egg, and vanilla until smooth. Stir in pancake mix until dough forms and mix is completely worked into the dough. Chill for 1 hour.

Preheat oven to 350 degrees.

Place sugar in a small bowl. Using a 1 tablespoon-size cookie scoop, drop dough into bowl and roll balls until coated. Place them on a baking sheet lightly prepared with nonstick cooking spray. Use a fork to make indentations in the dough. Cross the first indentation with another fork indentation. Bake for 8–10 minutes. Remove and allow cookies to cool. Makes 48 small cookies.

EASY SNICKERDOODLES

¹/₂ cup	**butter or margarine,** softened
³/₄ cup	**sugar**
1	**egg**
1 teaspoon	**vanilla**
1 ³/₄ cups	**pancake mix**
2 tablespoons	**sugar**
2 teaspoons	**cinnamon**

Preheat oven to 350 degrees.

In a 2-quart bowl, cream together butter and sugar. Mix in egg and vanilla. Stir in pancake mix until well blended. In a small bowl, combine sugar and cinnamon. Using a 1 tablespoon-size cookie scoop, drop dough into cinnamon and sugar mixture, roll, and place on baking sheet lightly prepared with nonstick cooking spray. Bake for 10–12 minutes. Makes 30 cookies.

CARAMEL, PEANUT, AND CHOCOLATE CHIP COOKIES

½ cup	**caramel ice cream topping**
½ cup	**crunchy peanut butter**
¼ cup	**butter or margarine,** softened
1	**egg**
1½ cups	**pancake mix**
¾ cup	**semisweet chocolate chips**

Preheat oven to 350 degrees.

In a 2-quart bowl, combine caramel, peanut butter, butter, and egg until blended. Stir in pancake mix until batter forms. Stir in chocolate chips. Using a 2 tablespoon-size cookie scoop, drop balls of dough onto a baking sheet lightly prepared with nonstick cooking spray. Bake for 10–12 minutes until light golden brown. Makes 24–26 cookies.

CANDY BAR COOKIES

1	**regular-size Butterfinger or Skor candy bar**
1	**regular-size Crunch or Mr. Goodbar candy bar**
1	**regular-size Milky Way or Whatchamacallit candy bar**
1 cup	**brown sugar**
1	**egg**
1/2 cup	**butter or margarine,** softened
2 teaspoons	**vanilla**
2 3/4 cups	**pancake mix**

Preheat oven to 350 degrees.

Chop or dice the candy bars. In a 2-quart bowl, mix together brown sugar, egg, butter, and vanilla until smooth. Mix in pancake mix until dough forms. Stir in candy. Using a 2 tablespoon-size cookie scoop, drop balls of dough onto an ungreased baking sheet. Bake for 10–12 minutes. Makes 30 cookies.

FRIED CHOCOLATE SANDWICH COOKIES

¹/₂ package (18 ounces)	**double-stuff chocolate sandwich cookies**
	vegetable or canola oil
1 cup	**pancake mix**
³/₄ cup	**cold water**
1 teaspoon	**vanilla**
	powdered sugar or chocolate syrup

Freeze cookies for 2–3 hours.

Heat oil in deep fryer or 4-quart saucepan to 375 degrees.

In a shallow bowl, whisk together pancake mix, water, and vanilla. Batter will be slightly lumpy.

Coat 4 cookies at a time in batter. Fry in hot oil for 1–2 minutes on each side until golden brown. Place cookies on a plate covered in paper towels. Repeat process for remaining cookies. Sprinkle powdered sugar or drizzle chocolate syrup over top. Makes 18 cookies.

COOKIE
PANCAKES A LA MODE

2 cups	**pancake mix**
1½ cups	**water**
20	**chocolate sandwich cookies,** finely chopped and divided
2 cups	**bananas,** sliced
2 cups	**fresh strawberries,** sliced
	vanilla ice cream or frozen yogurt
	caramel sauce

Heat an electric griddle to 350 degrees and prepare with nonstick cooking spray.

In a 2-quart bowl, whisk together pancake mix and water. Batter will be slightly lumpy. Fold in 1½ cups cookies. Pour ¼ cup batter per pancake evenly onto heated griddle. Cook for 1–2 minutes on each side until golden brown. Serve topped with bananas, strawberries, ice cream, caramel, and a sprinkle of remaining cookies. Makes 13 pancakes.

PEACH COBBLER

I can (29 ounces)	**peach slices,** drained, reserve juice
I cup	**pancake mix**
⅓ cup	**brown sugar**
	whipped cream or ice cream

Preheat oven to 375 degrees.

Place peach slices in a 8 x 8-inch pan prepared with nonstick cooking spray. In a I-quart bowl, combine pancake mix and brown sugar. Sprinkle pancake mixture evenly over top of peaches. Drizzle ½ cup of the reserved juice over the top. Bake uncovered for 40–45 minutes. Serve warm with whipped cream or ice cream. Makes 6 servings.

FRUIT COCKTAIL BUNDT CAKE

1 cup	**milk**
2	**eggs**
2 tablespoons	**olive oil**
1 cup	**brown sugar**
¾ cup	**applesauce**
1 teaspoon	**cinnamon**
1 teaspoon	**vanilla**
3 cups	**pancake mix**
1 can (15.25 ounces)	**fruit cocktail,** drained
	shortening
	powdered sugar

Preheat oven to 350 degrees.

In a 2-quart bowl, mix together milk, eggs, oil, sugar, applesauce, cinnamon, and vanilla until smooth. Mix in pancake mix one cup at a time. Cut the fruit into smaller pieces.

Grease a Bundt pan well with shortening. Pour half the batter evenly into pan. Layer half the fruit over batter. Pour remaining batter over the fruit. Sprinkle remaining fruit over the top. Bake for 45–50 minutes. While hot, invert onto a plate and allow to cool. Sprinkle powdered sugar over the top once cooled. Makes 12–15 servings.

GOOEY
CHOCOLATE CHERRY CAKE

Sauce:

I cup	**brown sugar**
1/3 cup	**unsweetened cocoa**
2 cups	**hot water**

Cake:

2 cups	**pancake mix**
3/4 cup	**sugar**
1/4 cup	**unsweetened cocoa**
2	**eggs**
1/4 cup	**olive or canola oil**
I teaspoon	**vanilla**
I can (21 ounces)	**cherry pie filling**

Preheat oven to 350 degrees.

Stir brown sugar, 1/3 cup cocoa, and hot water in the bottom of an ungreased 9 x 13-inch pan until sugar dissolves.

In a 2-quart bowl, combine pancake mix, sugar, and 1/4 cup cocoa. Stir in eggs, oil, vanilla, and pie filling until batter forms. Do not over mix. Spoon batter over sauce in pan. Bake for 35–40 minutes. Cut into squares and spoon sauce from bottom over individual servings. Makes 15 servings.

PECAN TOPPED PEACH CAKE

I	**egg**
³/₄ cup	**brown sugar**
¹/₂ cup	**milk**
I teaspoon	**cinnamon**
3 cups	**pancake mix**
I can (21 ounces)	**peach pie filling**
¹/₂ cup	**chopped pecans**

Preheat oven to 350 degrees.

In a 2-quart bowl, beat egg, and then whisk in brown sugar, milk, and cinnamon. Stir in pancake mix and pie filling until moistened. Spread cake batter into a 9 x 9-inch pan prepared with nonstick cooking spray. Sprinkle pecans over top of batter. Bake for 50 minutes, or until center of cake is set. Makes 9–12 servings.

NOTES

HELPFUL HINTS

1. There are a variety of pancake mixes to choose from at the store. To have the recipes work the best, use a pancake mix that calls only for water. I used Krusteaz Pancake Mix in all recipes.

2. Always remember to spray griddle or waffle makers with nonstick cooking spray before each new batch of pancakes or waffles to prevent sticking. If you don't have an electric griddle, invest in one. Check the ratings of various griddles on the Internet to determine which will work best for your family.

METRIC CONVERSION CHART

Volume Measurements		Weight Measurements		Temperature Conversion	
U.S.	Metric	U.S.	Metric	Fahrenheit	Celsius
1 teaspoon	5 ml	1/2 ounce	15 g	250	120
1 tablespoon	15 ml	1 ounce	30 g	300	150
1/4 cup	60 ml	3 ounces	90 g	325	160
1/3 cup	75 ml	4 ounces	115 g	350	180
1/2 cup	125 ml	8 ounces	225 g	375	190
2/3 cup	150 ml	12 ounces	350 g	400	200
3/4 cup	175 ml	1 pound	450 g	425	220
1 cup	250 ml	2 1/4 pounds	1 kg	450	230

 Check out these "101" favorites
for more tasty recipes:

Bacon	**Meatballs**
BBQ	**More Cake Mix**
Blender	**More Ramen**
Cake Mix	**More Slow Cooker**
Canned Biscuits	**Potato**
Canned Soup	**Pancake Mix**
Casserole	**Pudding**
Cheese	**Ramen Noodles**
Chicken	**Rotisserie Chicken**
Chocolate	**Salad**
Dutch Oven	**Slow Cooker**
Eggs	**Toaster Oven**
Gelatin	**Tofu**
Grits	**Tortilla**
Ground Beef	**Yogurt**
Mac & Cheese	**Zucchini**

Each 128 pages, $9.99

Available at bookstores or
directly from GIBBS SMITH
1.800.835.4993
www.gibbs-smith.com
101yum.com

ABOUT THE AUTHOR

Stephanie Ashcraft, author of *101 Things to Do with a Cake Mix*, along with fifteen other culinary offerings, has taught cooking classes based on the tips and meals in her cookbooks for over 13 years. She and her cookbooks have been featured on television and radio stations across the country.

Stephanie is always searching for ways to save time and money in the kitchen and she loves helping others to do the same. She has earned "Favorite Neighbor" status by sharing her culinary creations with those around her. She lives in Tucson, Arizona, with her husband and four children.